6 DECADES with Twelve

Bethany College Presidents

Student • Employee • Volunteer

by Kenneth Sjogren

© 2019 Kenneth Sjogren

All rights reserved. No portion of this book may be reproduced, stored in a retrieval system, or transmitted in any form or by any means – electronic, mechanical, photocopy, recording, scanning, or other – except for brief quotations in ritical reviews or articles, without the prior written permission of the publisher. Requests for permission should be addressed in writing to:
Kenneth Sjogren
210 W. Columbus
Lindsborg, KS 67456

ISBN: 978-1-944058-05-0

Acknowledgement

Dear Friends,

First, I must acknowledge my wife Marilyn, my Bethany College sweetheart from Littleton, Colorado. In my position of employment with the college, I traveled a great deal and Marilyn deserves much credit for raising our four children. I dedicate this book to my wife and family Karla Wright, Kristin Slater, Steven Sjogren, and Eric Sjogren, along with their families.

I also want to acknowledge the Bethany College Advancement Office for helping me retrieve information from the past decades of alumni magazines with a special thank you to Jane Asche, Secretary of the Advancement Office, for her assistance. Thanks to Jim Turner, Turner Photography for many of the photos. Other photos were retrieved from Bethany College files. Several individuals encouraged me to write this history which took place over the past six decades.

For the final make up of this history, I want to express my thanks and appreciation to Marty Schupbach, Editor and to Angeline Collier, Graphic Designer.

Table of Contents

Dr. Emory K. Lindquist 1941-1953 1

Dr. Robert Mortvedt 1953-1958 2

Dr. L. Dale Lund 1958-1965 4

Dr. G. Kenneth Andeen 1965-1967 7

Dr. Arvin Hahn 1967-1983 12

Dr. Peter Ristuben 1983-1990 34

Dr. Joel McKean 1991-1996 36

Rev. Christopher Thomforde 1996-2000 37

Dr. Paul Formo 2001-2006 38

Dr. Robert Vogel 2006 (6 months) 39

Dr. Edward Leonard III 2007-2015 40

Dr. Robert Vogel 2015-2016 43

President Will Jones 2016 44

Photo & Scrapbook Extras 46

Forward

This bit of history covers a span of six decades of my association with Bethany College, my alma mater; while I was a student, an employee, and a volunteer. I have done my best through both my memory and research, to cover my time spent with these 12 presidents. During these decades of history I had many unique experiences making my personal calls and I have included some of the most memorable. There are many other colleagues and individuals who could have been included in this history– I chose presidents. My association with Bethany includes:

Student	1953-1957, Bachelor of Arts degree
Employee	1961-1967 Director of Public Relations and Alumni Affairs
	1967-1984 Director of Development and Assistant to the President
Volunteer	1984-Present

Bethany College has had and continues to have a rich history and each of the 12 Presidents played an important role during his tenure. I hope you enjoy this walk through memory lane.

Kenneth Sjogren

Dr. Emory K. Lindquist 1941-1953

Dr. Emory Lindquist became the fourth president of Bethany College after serving on the faculty. He graduated from Bethany in 1930, was a Rhodes scholar from 1930–1933, and was awarded both BA and MA degrees from Oxford. In 1941, he earned his PhD in philosophy from the University of Colorado. He and his wife Irma had one son and one daughter.

Dr. Emory Lindquist was the president of Bethany College before my time as a student or an employee, but we developed a friendship in the 1960s when I was employed by the college and he was a real source of encouragement for me during the Andeen presidency.

Unsure of Bethany's future in Lindsborg, I called Dr. Lindquist, then president of Wichita University, for an appointment to ask his advice for the direction I should take during these uncertain times at our Alma Mater. He said "I'm leaving town for the University, but you can meet me at the Wichita air terminal and we can have a brief visit". What I remember most about this visit was his comment to me, "Ken, Bethany College needs you, and you must go out and make calls, calls, and more calls on behalf of our college." I took this admonition seriously, and it has been over a 50-year association of fun, trying times, and rewards both working and volunteering at Bethany.

Dr. Lindquist's love for his Alma Mater never dwindled during his lifetime. He always had time for Bethany and his home, Lindsborg, Kansas. In the 1950's, Dr. Lindquist became the president of Wichita University. It was under his leadership that Wichita University became Wichita State University.

Dr. Robert Mortvedt 1953-1958

Dr. Mortvedt became the fifth president of Bethany College. He earned his BA degree from St. Olaf College in Northfield, Minnesota, and later his PhD in English literature from Harvard. Prior to coming to Bethany as president, he was professor of English, Dean of the College of Liberal arts and sciences, and vice president of the University of Kansas City. In 1958, at the end of his service to Bethany, Dr. Mortvedt became president of Pacific Lutheran College in Tacoma, Washington where he and his wife Gladys later retired. The Mortvedt's had one daughter.

I remember Dr. Robert Mortvedt as a highly educated individual who was very serious and fair. He was the president during my four years as a student from 1953–1957. I had several occasions to be in his office because I was student body president and a fraternity president during his tenure. Both of these student offices required visits to the presidents office for one reason or another– some good, some not so good. Dr. Mortvedt, as I have said, earned his PhD from Harvard University and he acquired a Boston accent during his four years. As I recall, many of the local midwestern boys had a difficult time understanding him.

Facilities built under his administration were the dormitory Deere Hall, Nelson Science Hall, and the Birger Sandzen Memorial Gallery. Over the years alumni and friends wondered why the bricks on Nelson Science Hall were ivory rather than red. It was very simple, Mrs. Selma Nelson liked ivory bricks and she was the president of the Ludwig and Selma Nelson Charitable Trust which contributed the major gift for this building.

Nelson Science Hall

Dr. Mortvedt was an avid sportsman. As president of the student body, I needed all the "points" I could accrue. I knew of some good hunting areas just below Kanopolis Reservoir and it was great for duck hunting in the winter. Courageously, I asked our president if he would like to go duck hunting. He was very appreciative and accepted the invitation. Unfortunately, I was a student who had only a thin fraternity jacket and a shotgun like a "BB" gun. Dr. Mortvedt, however, had all the good hunting equipment from the outerwear to the shotgun. As we lay in the duck blind in a cornfield, with the snow, ducks flying overhead, I was so cold I could not pull the trigger on my gun! President Mortvedt did make his kill. I was happy to take my president hunting, but much happier to get home where it was warm.

In 1956 a very special person came into my life and her name was Marilyn Miller, a Bethany student from Littleton, Colorado. She became my dear wife in 1958 and we have now been together for 60 years. We were blessed with two daughters Karla and Kristin and two sons Steven and Eric. Now there are eight grandchildren.

Dr. Mortvedt faced financial difficulties during his tenure at Bethany College but the students were unaware there was a problem. The small student body was very happy, we had good professors, and the food was good under the leadership of Mrs. Thorstenberg and her staff. Many of our students found our spouses while at Bethany and also received a good education. Dr. Mortvedt resigned as president of Bethany in 1958 taking a new position as the president of Pacific Lutheran University in Tacoma Washington.

Birger Sandzen Memorial Gallery

AUTHOR'S ANECDOTES

Our student body had a great men's quartet that performed many places and on many occasions. The students loved their music. We had an exchange chapel program among our Kansas Conference schools and we were invited to perform at Bethel College in North Newton. As Student Body President, I introduced the program. The quartet sang music of the 50s and it was very good, however, very loud and Bethel College might have been too conservative for this program. It was even more difficult for us because the faculty members were on the front rows and our music did not come from a red hymnal! Guess who is waiting for me when we got home? I was to report to Dr. Mortvedt's office right away. He shared that the feelings of the Bethel College faculty with me who had reported the music was not appropriate.

My friend Ron Moore and I were both from Marquette, Kansas and we wanted to play football for the Swedes in the worst way. We were very excited that the Lindsborg Quarterback Club thought enough of us that they presented us a $125.00 scholarship only to find out later that this was illegal; we had to give the money back. This was my first introduction to Bethany.

Dr. L. Dale Lund 1958-1965

Dr. L. Dale Lund became the sixth president of Bethany College coming from Uppsala College in East Orange, New Jersey. There he served as chaplain and associate professor of Christianity. He earned his BA degree from Gustavus Adolphus College in St. Peter, Minnesota and his PhD from Drew University in Madison, New Jersey. Dr. Lund and his wife Ruth had four children. After leaving Bethany in 1965 he became president of the Lutheran School of Theology in Chicago and later president of Midland College in Fremont, Nebraska, where he retired.

Dr. Lund was very special to me personally. He offered me the opportunity to go to work at Bethany as an employee. On May 15, 1961, I accepted the position of Director of Public Relations and the Alumni Program. Under Dr. Lund's leadership, he continued to carry out a program that was started under Dr. Morvedt's administration. During his years at Bethany, the college witnessed a substantial growth in full-time enrollment. Three hundred airmen from Schilling Air Force Base in Salina, Kansas took courses offered by the college on a part-time basis.

Under Dr. Lund's leadership six new facilities were added to the campus and community. These additions included the Ray D. Hahn physical education building, Anna Marm residence hall, Deere Hall addition, Pihlblad Memorial Union, a football stadium with track, and the president's home. The first of these additions was the Hahn physical education building which included a varsity gymnasium, a classroom, dressing rooms, and faculty offices. During Coach Hahn's many years at Bethany, he coached football, basketball, track, and tennis. His wife Mildred spent many hours mending uniforms for all the sports. The new women's dorm that was built was named Anna Marm Hall in honor of Miss Marm who graduated from Bethany and taught mathematics here for 33 years.

Ray D. Hahn Physical Education Building

The third building completed was Pihlblad Memorial Union named in honor of Dr. and Mrs. Ernst Pihlblad. Dr. Pihlblad was also a graduate of Bethany and served as president from 1904-1941. The Student Union, as it was known, housed the dining room, offices, bookstore, recreation area, and the college post office. Dr. Lund also completed the second addition to Deere Hall to handle the growing enrollment. This dorm was named in honor of Dr. Emil O. Deere, Professor of Biology and a 1904 graduate of Bethany. The next structure to be completed was the Philip Anderson football field, the result of a gift of land from Philip Anderson of Lindsborg Kansas. This football field and new stadium were surrounded by a new cinder track. The final structure added to the college was a new larger home built for the president on the 600 block on North Washington Street. This home was built for the staff, students and campus visitors. Presidents Lund, Andeen, Hahn, and Ristuben called this their home. Following Dr. Ristuben the college sold this home and no longer owned a president's home.

Dr. Lund was a change agent and in the fall of 1960 a very important action took place for the faculty and administration's welfare. The Board of Directors authorized and helped to fund participation in the Teachers' Insurance and Annuity Association known among colleges throughout the country as "TIAA". This joint contribution plan for faculty and college was a proper recognition of their welfare and a decisive step in retaining and recruiting both faculty and administration. Dr. Lund coordinated another significant change to make Bethany a College of Liberal Arts and Sciences. Prior to this, the academic year of 1962-1963, Bethany had two major divisions; the College of Liberal Arts and the College of Fine Arts. This change took place after much discussion. It was at this time that Dr. Albert A. Zimmer, Professor of Education and Dean of Students at Susquehanna University in Pennsylvania became Bethany's new Academic Dean.

Anna Marm Residence Hall

These years proved to be very positive for long range resources. Endowment funds increased and in 1964-1965, the college assets doubled. This was the greatest single development in a similar span of years in Bethany's history. The total indebtedness was $1.1 million which included $975,000 in the plant fund and $205,000 in the current fund accumulated over many years. Following the 1965 academic year, Dr. Lund took a call to become the Dean of the Lutheran School of Theology in Chicago and later became President of Midland Lutheran College in Fremont Nebraska where he retired.

Pihlblad Memorial Union

AUTHOR'S ANECDOTES

Dr. Lund offered me the position of Director of Public Relations and Alumni Affairs in the spring of 1961; I accepted his invitation. Marilyn and I were excited about my new position of employment. On May 15, 1961, I met my predecessor Elwood Landes, in the foyer of Presser Hall. I was looking forward to him showing me my office and meeting my secretary. Mr. Landes said to me," Sjogren, you are a damned fool." He handed me the keys and left. This was my introduction to my first day of work at Bethany College.

Dr. G. Kenneth Andeen 1965-1967

Dr. Andeen became the seventh president of Bethany College, coming from Rockford College, Rockford, Illinois, where he was chairman of the Division of Religion and Philosophy. Andeen earned his BA degree from Uppsala College in New Jersey, and his PhD in Religion from Columbia University in New York City. Dr. Andeen and his wife Constance had two sons and a daughter.

When Dr. G. Kenneth Andeen became the seventh president of Bethany College, it didn't take long to learn that he was a history buff. Our travels took us to several museums on our trips. Several months after he became president I took him to visit several alumni clubs around the country. Our first trip was heading west to California. Our travels took us to San Diego, Los Angeles, San Francisco, Seattle, then on to Minnesota. We also visited many funding prospects along with our meetings. When we returned to campus, Dr. Andeen asked me, " Where is all the money?" I told him this was his introduction to our alumni to help open doors for the future. Several months later, three alumni meetings were set up in Colorado; Longmont, Denver, and Colorado Springs. By now at least 18 months had passed in Andeen's presidency. I was joined on this trip to Colorado by my wife Marilyn and our two young daughters. Marilyn's parents lived in Englewood, Colorado, and they were able to take care of our children. The Colorado Springs meeting was our last in the mountains. Mr. Gunner Alenius, a Bethany board member and controller of the famous Broadmoor Hotel, had complementary rooms for Dr. and Mrs. Andeen and for us. Our room faced the mountains and on the dresser was a vase of flowers and a bottle of wine. As a young couple with a young family, we hardly ever had an overnight out together, and especially at a place like the Broadmoor. Soon our phone rang and it was President Andeen, and he said "Why don't you and Marilyn come down to our room for a dish of ice cream?" While we were enjoying our ice cream treat together, President Andeen asked us, 'What do you think Joe Levin, a Lindsborg businessman, would think if we moved the college to Colorado?" Marilyn

The Wichita Eagle

Marcellus M. Murdock
Chairman of the Board and President

Britt Brown
Vice President and Secretary

John H. Colburn
Editor and Publisher

Founded in 1872 by Marshall M. Murdock

Page 4A   EDITORIAL OPINION PAGE   Monday, February 27, 1967

Kansas Has a Stake In Keeping Bethany at Lindsborg

Bethany College is one of Kansas' finest assets. It is good to learn that an effort will be made to insure that it stays in Lindsborg and to upgrade it. (A story on page 1B of Sunday's paper told about this effort.) Rumors have been circulating for months that the college would be moved or might even close.

Such a thing should never be allowed to happen.

Bethany's departure would be a severe economic and psychological blow to Lindsborg and the surrounding area, of course. But, in addition, the loss would be felt throughout the state.

Bethany's influence is unique among small colleges. It has enriched education in Kansas because hundreds of its graduates are teaching in our state's schools. It is an impressive cultural resource. Its adjuncts, the annual Messiah festival and the Birger Sandzen Memorial Art Gallery, have done much to dispel the notion that Kansas is a cultural desert. The college undoubtedly has been an encouragement to artists who have settled in Lindsborg. And it has been a factor in the preservation of the Swedish heritage that makes Lindsborg such a stimulating place.

Bethany and Lindsborg, inseparable during two centuries, are known far and wide. Their fame enhances the image of Kansas.

A major problem of the school is to get its financing on a sound long-range basis. And really no one but the college and the community can provide the leadership for solving this. But now that they are facing up to the problem, and are taking steps to make known the school's needs, they may find they have more friends and will receive more help than they suspected. Surely there are many Kansans, and persons in other states, too, who have no direct connection with Bethany but who would offer assistance to keep it in Lindsborg and to improve it.

Pride and sentiment aside, our state as a whole has a real stake in the preservation of Bethany. Kansas is concerned about providing education for its growing number of college-age people. We need all the colleges and universities we can get. Private colleges like Bethany can play an important role in higher education. Even with its present facilities and faculty, Bethany could accommodate at least 200 more students.

In an official capacity, the state probably could not or would not want to offer direct aid to Bethany. But there is before the Kansas House of Representatives a bill that would provide tuition grants, ranging up to $500 a year, to students enrolling in private colleges. Such assistance actually would cost the state less than if it had to accommodate these students in state schools. The grants would help private colleges by encouraging students to attend them. The Bethany situation is another reason why legislators should look with favor on the tuition grant bill.

---

and I were stunned by this question. Dr. Andeen had already done a lot of work with a Colorado Springs member of our Board of Directors, the former governor of Iowa, Leo Hoegh. It was hard to believe that a site had already been selected for the move. Of course, we were not in favor of this shocking news. I believe we were the first in the Bethany family Dr. Andeen told of his plan. However, it wasn't long until the campus and the Lindsborg community heard the news of a potential move. Needless to say this news created a great deal of upheaval on campus and it wasn't long until Dr. Andeen was forced to have his office in the basement of the president's home. Phone calls were coming to the college office from everywhere. The days and weeks ahead became difficult for everyone, including my position as Director of Public Relations and Alumni Affairs. Alumni were calling me to ask what was going on with the president and moving the college to Colorado. Dr. Elmer Peterson, Bethany alumnus and former editor of the Daily Oklahoman in Oklahoma City, said "Moving Bethany College to Colorado would be like moving Plymouth Rock to the center of Kansas. It would be the same rock, but have a different meaning!" Now, the Kansas news and media from Salina, Hutchinson, Topeka, and Wichita we're sharing the news with full page articles. Soon, editorials appeared in the major print media. One editorial stated, "Kansas has stake in keeping Bethany in Lindsborg!" All the news events on the outside we're putting pressure internally on the Bethany family. The campus, of course, wondered what was going to happen next. Some faculty and administrtatioin did not know how to feel about the news. Do any of us have job security? Bethany students were stalwarts during this whole ordeal; they wanted Bethany to stay right in Lindsborg. Although the news was shocking to everyone, Dr. Andeen was a friend of the students. The Student Congress appreciated the president's integrity and honesty after he held a series of free discussions, including some frank criticism and debate, which were a highlight in the eyes of Bethany students.

During this period of time a study was requested by the Board of Directors in accordance with the policy of the board of education of the Lutheran Church in America. This study was made under the direction Dr. Francis Gamelin, Executive Director of the LCA Board of Education, and was presented in 1966. It dealt with the college's objectives, faculty, student life, facilities, administration, government, costs, and financing significant survival. Emphasis in this report was placed on the consequences of prolonged financial problems and was a real eyeopener. Some pressure was put to rest as Dr. Axel Beckman, chairman of the Board, identified this action in his report to the Kansas Conference of the Lutheran Church in America April 1967 with these words, " An ill-conceived effort to pre-evaluate the findings of the status study precipitated unfounded rumors of Bethany's removal to another location". The board of directors at this time included members from different areas of the church, alumni, and friends, from the states of Missouri, Kansas, Colorado, Oklahoma, and New Mexico. After meeting on campus, there was great pressure when a vote was taken to move the college or to keep it in Lindsborg. As I remember, the vote was taken toward the end of the meeting and some members from a great distance had to leave early for transportation connections. The Board of Directors then voted and the decision was made to keep Bethany in Lindsborg. The vote was close. Dr. Andeen resigned as president on February 9, 1967. He was a very kind man, who I believe, did a favor for Lindsborg

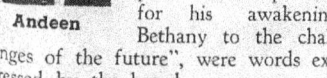

Andeen Submits Resignation at Meeting

The resignation of Dr. G. Kenneth Andeen, President of Bethany College since July, 1965 was accepted at the February 7, 1967 meeting of the Board of Directors. The announcement was made by Rev. Axel Beckman, Kansas City, president of the board.

"We express our deep appreciation to Dr. Andeen for his past leadership and for his awakening Bethany to the challenges of the future", were words expressed by the board.

Named to head the administration of the college during the vacancy created by Dr. Andeen's resignation is Dr. Albert A. Zimmer, Dean and Vice-President of the college. He will be assisted by an administrative committee consisting of representation from the board of directors, the community, and the administrative council.

Dr. Conrad Bergendoff, former president of Augustana College of Rock Island, Illinois is a consultant to the administration and the board of directors during the vacancy.

through the Bethany College family by suggesting a move to Colorado. The college should not be taken for granted. Dr. Albert A. Zimmer, Academic Dean appointed by Dr. Lund, became acting president. Director of Development Vernon Johnson had resigned earlier to go into business in Nebraska. The next major step was a town hall meeting held the first week of April 1967 in Presser

Hall Auditorium. Approximately 700 alumni and friends attended this meeting with Dr. Walter Ostenberg, a 1924 graduate and former superintendent of Salina Central High School, and currently vice president of National Bank of America, as the keynote speaker. This Town hall meeting was set up by Jack Carlin, a Lindsborg resident, Bethany College Board member and chairman of this special campaign to have funds raised to meet current operating expenses. Dr. Ostenberg challenged the Lindsborg businesses and community, saying they now had a stake in this very unique place called Bethany College. This evening was very special, and I truly believe God was looking down on all of us. We had tables set up in the Presser Hall foyer with pledge cards from the previous campaign marked SPECIAL. During the evening the heavens broke loose and it poured down rain; no one could leave Presser Hall. This was a great opportunity to have everyone sign pledge cards. By 10:30 pm, everyone had signed their pledge cards and I had the great opportunity to call the Associated Press with a total of $82,000 raised that evening! Many members of our community made sacrificial gifts. Several took out loans from the bank, and I know one alum that evening who gave up buying a new car to make his gift.

Yes, this was a new beginning for Bethany. After all was said and done, even difficult times, we can look back and again say Dr. Andeen did Lindsborg and Bethany College a real favor.

AUTHOR'S ANECDOTES

The Lindsborg community really got the message. Alumni and friends dug deeply to help the college financially. One of my friends, Dale Hoag, was visiting Hilding Jaderborg at the Swedish Crafts on Main Street. When Mr. Hoag saw me coming into the store, and he was young enough to hide under a table. I did see him and I said "Dale, I want you to consider a $1000 gift." Dale said "I will give you a $1000 gift if you can get Mr. Abercrombie, president of Farmers State Bank, to draw up a loan." I went over to Abercrombie at the bank and he agreed to draw up the papers for the loan. I went back to Swedish Crafts and told Dale that the loan papers were ready to sign!

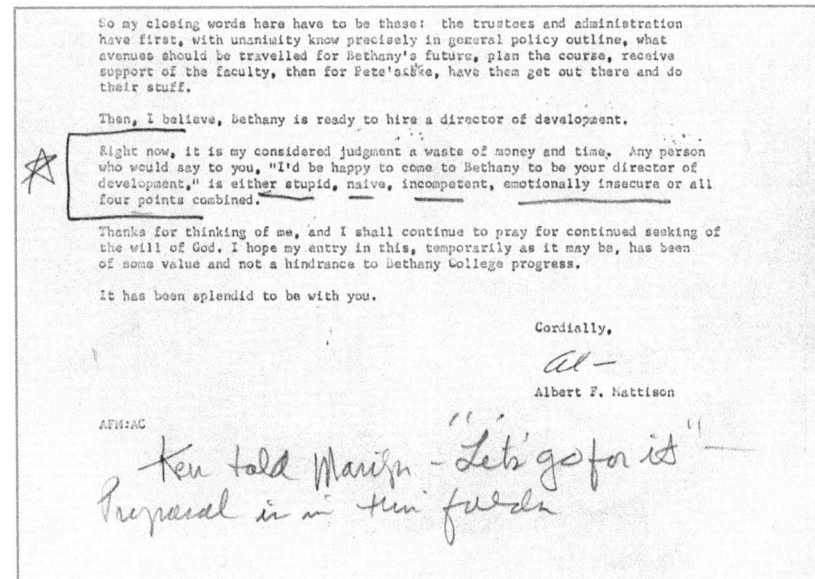

So now it was time to set up the search committee for a new president and a new Development Director. Dr. Axel Beckman, Board Chairman, called Albert Mattison in New Hampshire and requested him to visit Bethany to consider the Development Director's position. I picked him up at the Wichita airport terminal and he visited the campus. Upon returning home, he wrote Dr. Beckman that he was not interested. In the last paragraph of his letter, Mr. Mattison wrote, "any one person who would say to you, I'd be happy to come to Bethany as your Director of Development, is either stupid, naïve, incompetent, emotionally insecure, or all four points combined".

Dr. Andeen told me earlier that I should get my advanced degree to be a development director in higher education. Because I was young and uncertain about my position, I applied and was accepted at Southern Illinois University. Our house was for sale for one week. After reading the last line of Albert Mattison's letter, I told Marilyn, "This is a challenge, let's go for it!" After writing a proposal to apply for the Director of Development position, I contacted Dr. Beckman. I believe the Board of Directors were so happy someone wanted to tackle this position I was made the new acting Director of Development. Now it was time for our next educator to accept the position as the eighth president of Bethany College.

AUTHOR'S ANECDOTES

Bryce Nelson a reporter for the Los Angeles Times, came to do a story on Gov. Alf Landon. Gov. Landon was ill and Nelson's appointment was canceled. Fortunately, someone tipped Bryce Nelson about the success story happening at Bethany College in Lindsborg. Nelson came to the campus and interviewed several of us about the community coming to the aid of the college. After the interview at the city bakery, and sharing, our story appeared the next day on the front page of the Los Angeles Times. The article had the headline "Small Town Comes to the Aid of Their College". They gave us several inches of space this was another article for Bethany and Lindsborg in the print media.

Dr. Arvin Hahn 1967-1983

Dr. Arvin Hahn became Bethany's eighth president, coming from Concordia Teachers College in River Forest, Illinois. A graduate of Concordia College, he earned his PhD from Northwestern University. Dr. Hahn was also a member of the Public Relations and Television Committees of the Missouri Synod Lutheran Church. Dr. Hahn and his wife Judie had two sons and a daughter.

As the eighth president, Dr. Hahn soon won respect both on the campus and in the larger community for his ability, vision, and dedication to Christian Higher Education.

Dr. Albert Zimmer, acting President and Academic Dean, had now resigned to become Academic Dean at Thiel College returning to Pennsylvania. Dr. Lloyd Forrester, of Concordia College and a close friend of President Hahn, came to Bethany to become Academic Dean. In a very short time, President Hahn began to assign priorities for the academic program and campus facilities. His determination as the new president was to fulfill the items left from the 1966 study by the division of higher education of the Lutheran Church in America (LCA) under the Dr. Andeen presidency. Dr. Hahn put together an administrative team who worked well together. Student enrollment and fund-raising were now on the increase.

My position was now Director of Development and this left a void in the Public Relations and the Alumni program. L. Stanley Talbott, a member of the Bethany Alumni Council and a 1946 graduate, always said "if you ever need any help, please call me." He lived in Russell, Kansas, where he was the band director at Russell High School. I called Stan just as he was ready to accept the band director position at Butler Community College in El Dorado, Kansas. "Stan, remember when you said call you when we needed help?" I said, "Stan, we need you to become our Director of Public Relations and Alumni Programs." There was a silence, and he said "I'll let you know tomorrow." He did let us know, and accepted the position. He instantly became known as "Mr. Bethany" to all the alumni for many years. I continued, "Also, Stan, would your wife Pauline have an interest in becoming Dean of Women?" Pauline (Pennington), a 1942 graduate of Bethany, became our Dean of Women and these two outstanding alums served their alma mater and the Lindsborg community for nearly 2 decades. This all happened in 1967. By now, Dean Forrester had set up faculty committees to enhance the academic program.

Dr. Emory Lindquist, in his book Bethany in Kansas, pointed out that the Hahn era was "a miracle in the making." Pres. Hahn hired Shaffer Architects of Salina, Kansas to draw up plans for a library, classroom building, and residence hall. The library and classroom building were to encircle a walkway to be known as "the million-dollar circle." The other facility in this plan was a two story residence hall.

Everything was happening very quickly. Old Main, built in 1886, neglected over the years, and in bad condition, could not feasibly be renovated. This building stood five stories tall and was once the tallest building between Kansas City and Denver; now it was scheduled to come down. Of course many of the older alumni who slept, attended chapel, ate their meals, and attended classes in

AUTHOR'S ANECDOTES

In the mid 70s, we were fund raising for a new organ in Presser Hall Auditorium. As written in the Hahn era, the Julia J. Mingenback Foundation and Mr. Carl Thompson made the major gifts. However, additional funds were needed. Looking through the foundation directory, I noticed that John Stupp Foundation in St. Louis had made a gift to a Lutheran Hospital. Just maybe this could be a prospect for the new organ. I called Mr. Stupp, President of Stupp Brothers Bridge and Iron Company. I gave my name and noted his foundation had given to a Lutheran Hospital, and that he might be Lutheran. Mr. Stupp said "No, I am not Lutheran." I asked Mr. Stupp if he had ever heard about Bethany College in Kansas he had not and I was about to lose him." Mr. Stupp, will you give me three minutes on the phone?" And he said yes. Then he told me to send a letter, and I followed through with my request. I received a return letter from Mr. Stupp and he wrote, "A blind pig occasionally finds an acorn. Enclosed is $1000." I thought the short note was neat and even better that he gave a gift. The next year I wrote Mr. Stupp a letter for $1000 and signed the letter "The Blind Pig." Again, I received $1000. This went on for a few years. Finally, on a round trip from Detroit, I made an appointment to meet this John Stupp. He had a very large business and we had lunch in his cafeteria. We stayed in touch until I resigned from the college in 1984.

Top: Old Main

Bottom Left: Demolition of Lane Hart Hall

Bottom Right: Demolition of Old Main

Old Main were somewhat upset. Ironically, Old Main was much harder to demolish than the team running the one ton wrecking ball had anticipated! The new library plans we're now completed at an estimated cost of $700,000 with one third of the funds coming from a federal government grant. There was now a need for an additional $470,000 from a private source.

Mr. Alvar Wallerstedt, a 1916 graduate of the Bethany College Commercial Department, became a high ranking accountant in private industry. He was associated with a prominent legal firm in Pittsburgh, Pennsylvania. He later became a director of North American Rockwell Corporation along with other directorships in several other corporations. He seemed to be a prospect for the new library in spite of the fact he had told our office that he would make his $500 dollar gift each year and there was no need to come and see him for an additional gift. Mr. Wallerstedt had a good friend in Lindsborg, Mr. Joe Levin. He too was a Bethany College Commercial graduate and classmate of Mr. Wallerstedt. I went to see Mr. Levin and asked," if we were to go to Mr. Wallerstedt for a gift, how much do you think he might consider giving?" I was told he was on many corporate boards and owned thousands of shares in the stock market. " I think he should give at least $15,000", said Mr. Levin. Well, you don't tell a Development Director all this information without the calculator starting to click. It made sense we should name the library after the Wallerstedts and go for $470,000, two thirds of the library cost estimate. Dr. Hahn felt the amount might be too much and we should go for $250,000. However, we convinced the president to go for the full proposal for the library and classroom building.

AUTHOR'S ANECDOTES

Many of us remember the small Hytone writing tablets like our parents used. A short letter came to my desk and it was a two liner with the following " Dear Sir: I would like to make a $90,000 gift to Bethany College if I can get a tax deduction." Signed Grace Gregory I called her immediately and told her," of course you can make a gift to Bethany College and you can receive a deduction." I set up an appointment for two days later and looked forward to meeting Mrs. Gregory. The next morning, Grace called me and said," you better come over and get the money today because I don't feel good." This was not good news to me and I immediately checked out a vehicle and headed to Lyons, Kansas. I was there in just over one hour. Mrs. Gregory and I had a good visit and we went to the bank and took care of business. At this time, there was a need for a coed residence hall, so Dr. Hahn and I took the architect's drawings which we had, added some color, and shared the residence hall drawings with Mrs. Gregory. She liked the idea for a Gregory Hall. Other gifts were added to hers and made Gregory Hall possible.

Of course there needed to be a special gathering (cultivation in development) so that President Hahn and his wife Judie would at least know the Wallerstedts. Alvar and Forrest Wallerstedt were invited back for Homecoming in the fall of 1968 and the Hahns and Wallerstedts were together briefly for this social occasion. Carl Nelson, a member of the Bethany College Board of Directors from Wichita, and President Hahn set up an appointment in January with the Wallerstedts at their winter home in Palm Beach, Florida. The proposal written for them carried a simple message of how their gift would be a turning point in the history of Bethany College. Dr. Hahn and Mr. Nelson were off to visit the Wallerstedts. During this social visit, the prepared library proposal was presented for $470,000 and Mr. Wallerstedt told the president that he was getting a little presumptuous. The visit went well and the next day was strictly a social. Three weeks later, I happened to be in Dr. Hahn's office just before lunch. President Hahn said, "I think I will call Alvar and see what the weather is like in Florida." Mr. Wallerstedt said, "Arvin, you're getting a little edgy, aren't you? Forrest and I have decided not to give you $470,000; we want to give you $500,000, but you must match this gift." The Central States Synod of the Lutheran Church in America was a big part of matching the Wallerstedt challenge. You can imagine the exuberance we all felt about this great news. William Taylor, business manager, was immediately called into the president's office to hear the news. We made a pact between all of us: if the news leaked out we would lose our jobs. Obviously, we kept it a secret for several reasons.

Remember, there was a $250,000 debt inherited from the previous administrations. President Hahn told the community that we have the biggest news ever to be announced at Bethany if we can eliminate this debt. So during a cold February, we had breakfast at 6:30 AM every morning for 10 days in the AAL Dining Room of the Student Union. A small group of community

AUTHOR'S ANECDOTES

Oscar Nelson was a self-made Swedish businessman from humble beginnings who became president and CEO of Butler Manufacturing in Kansas City. Oscar started to work for Mr. Butler at a young age. Later in life, when Oscar was older, I took Marilyn, our daughters Karla and Kristin, and our two sons Steven and Eric, to visit Mr. Nelson in the Trinity Lutheran Manor Home. Oscar was a dear friend and opened many doors for me in Kansas City. During our visit Oscar said," boys, jump up on my bed. I want to tell you a story. He told the boys that he had started to work for Mr. Butler at a salary of $5.65 a week. "I kept working for Butler Manufacturing, being an office boy, delivering mail to offices, and eventually worked my way up to president and CEO of the company, making well over $100,000 a year. Then your daddy came and took all my money away from me." He was a wonderful man.

Wallerstedt Learning Center

individuals were invited each morning. Jack Carlin, a member of the board from Lindsborg, headed each breakfast and no one left the breakfast each morning without signing a pledge. After totaling the pledges from the breakfast and adding a grant from the Ludwig and Selma Nelson Trust, we met the goal of $250,000.

A Town Hall Meeting was scheduled to make the promised big announcement. It seemed the community was used to Town Hall meetings and this one was also held in Presser Hall Auditorium. President Hahn announced, to a very large crowd, the large debt had been eliminated! The next announcement was the $500,000 challenge gift from Alvar and Forest Wallerstedt for the new library. The announcements took 15 minutes and everyone was invited to the Pihlblad Memorial Union for dessert where the celebration began. This event turned the college around from a negative to a positive feeling which had been absent for a very long time.

More changes were happening quickly. This was the plan for the coming year:
1. A new library and classroom facility will be built. Mr. and Mrs. Paul Nels Carlson of Seattle, Washington, made a major pledge for this classroom facility.
2. Two older facilities will be moved to the Old Mill Historical Park, The Swedish Pavilion which housed the Art Department and the first classroom building on campus which currently served to house maintenance.
3. Old Main would be coming down.
4. Swensson Street would be closed through the campus. Dr. Hahn has asked the city to have this street closed because there were safety concerns for the students. Swensson ran right through the center of campus; the vacant street would be renamed the Miller-Stromquist Mall honoring the donation made by Mr. and Mrs. Carl Miller of Longmont, Colorado. The farmers were not happy, as it closed their direct route from the east to the west part of town.
5. A new three-story residence hall was in the master plan. Mr. and Mrs. Walter Warner of Salina, Kansas, made a significant gift, which, along with a government grant, made Warner Hall possible.

I remember a very unusual call made on the J.M. McDonald Foundation in Hastings, Nebraska. Professor Ray Kahmeyer, chairman of the Art Department, needed pottery wheels for the ceramics department. Professor Kahmeyer and I had an appointment with Mr. McDonald and arrived for our meeting on time. I remember Mr. McDonald could hardly be seen because his office was so long. Our proposal was for only $3500. Mr. McDonald said, "Gentlemen, we are already committed and I don't think we can help your college, "Then he said, "You don't need much for your project, and we will help you purchase these pottery wheels." We, of course, felt good about our call and thanked him for his time. As we started to leave, he said, "I would like to visit your campus." We said we would certainly welcome his visit and then we left. About two weeks later, Dr. Hahn was on his way to the Student Union when a small yellow sports car stopped President Hahn and asked to see Mr. "Sjoo." He couldn't pronounce my name. Dr. Hahn got in touch with me and Professor Kahmeyer and told us we needed to get over to the ceramics laboratory and he would have the McDonalds meet us at the Art Department site. The ceramics lab was housed in the same facility as the college athletic dressing room and was not at all attractive or efficient. Jim McDonald looked through the door and said, "Well, hell, this equipment won't even fit in this room. You better build a new building." The J.M. McDonald Foundation made a $100,000 pledge toward a new art facility! Luckily we had already become friends with Mrs. Mary Mingenback and the board of the Julia J. Mingenback Foundation of McPherson, Kansas. A proposal was written and I delivered it to Mary Mingenback who was the president. This request was for $100,000 and she felt the board would go along with the request. Thus the next big accomplishment, the Mingenback Arts Center would become a reality.

AUTHOR'S ANECDOTES

A trip to Kansas City with Marilyn and our two small girls, Karla and Kristin, was a treat. Yes it was also business. Mrs. Grant Stauffer, a 1910 graduate, wanted to meet my family and we made an appointment for the visit. Mrs. Stauffer lived in the Kansas City Plaza in a large apartment facility called the "Walnuts". We arrive to our location on time and met the door man named Sandy. Sandy said" Mrs. Stauffer will be back soon and you are to wait in the parlor." Our girls got to know Sandy quickly and he gave them rides up and down the elevator. When Mrs. Stauffer arrived we went up to her apartment and she shared some little surprises with the girls. We had a nice visit and when it was time to leave, we got in our car, and Karla said," Daddy we wouldn't be here if she didn't have money, would we?" It didn't take long for my family to see what my job entailed.

Excerpt from 1970 Day of Dedication Brochure

October 18, 1970, was a "Day of Dedication." On this special day the college dedicated the Walllerstedt Library, Wallerstedt Social Science Center, Warner Residence Hall, and the Mingenback Arts Center. Major funds had been raised from the Mabee Foundation, Kresge Foundation, and several other individuals that covered the costs of all these facilities making them debt free.

Things were moving so rapidly that we felt the need to hire a Director of Public Relations to relieve L. Stanley Talbott of the double duty in Public Relations and Alumni Affairs. I felt I knew the perfect person for this job. A. John Pearson was in similar work at Illinois College in Eureka, Illinois. I remembered John as a student at Bethany in his freshman and sophomore years. He owned a large camera and took great pictures. In August 1970, John and his wife Carol arrived on campus to take over Public Relations. Also, during this time frame, James Attleson of Denver, Colorado, active in the insurance field, joined our Public Affairs staff in Planned Giving.

On October 2, 1972, Bethany announced an $11,055,000 nine-year Centennial Decade Development Program to culminate in 1981. Momentum was now in our favor and there was no time to rest. To assist in this effort, a

AUTHOR'S ANECDOTES

It was a beautiful day in May when Arvin Hahn and I accepted an invitation to be guests of Charles Dean Johnson on Kanopolis Lake to go fishing. First, I must tell you that Arvin Hahn was not a fisherman, and neither was I. At Kanopolis Lake, Charles Dean lived with a fishing pole in his hands and a shotgun on his shoulder. First, we went in the boat down the river below a tunnel and in less than 10 minutes, Dr. Hahn did not duck under a low tree limb and his glasses ended up in the river. That ended our evening fishing trip. The next morning we went trolling for fish in front of the dam in Johnson's large pontoon boat. The weather was changing and the clouds in the west were purple; it looked bad. The wind came up and those of us on the boat told Charlie we needed to get back. He wanted to troll one more time. We were bouncing around like a rubber ball. All of us had lifejackets. Dr. Hahn said, "Ken, can I have your lifejacket?" I said no because you have your own. It was back to the cabin, then back to work. Caught no fish.

Burnett Center for Religion and Performing Arts

President's Advisory Council made up of 30 distinguished business and professional leaders was appointed to facilitate this program. Mr. and Mrs. Alvar Wallerstedt, Pittsburgh, Pennsylvania, served as honorary co-chairman. Mr. Ed Bittner, Vice Chairman of the Board of First National Bank in Kansas City, Missouri, was chairman of the Centennial Decade Development Program and Lester Woodward, attorney in Denver, became chairman of the Annual Funding. Robert Sunderland, chairman of the Board of Ash Grove Cement Company, headed the Capital Funding. Russ B. Anderson, attorney in Emporia, Kansas, headed the Endowment Funding.

The Burnett Center for Religion and Performing Arts was the next new building to be added to the campus thanks to a gift of $200,000 from Gene and Barbara Burnett of Lawrence, Kansas. Mr. Burnett started the Burnett Instrument Company, a manufacturer of medical products. It was at this time that Dr. Elmer Copley, Professor of Music and Choir Director, took the choir on a tour of the East Coast. The highlight of the tour was their concert in the Alice Tully Hall in Lincoln Center, New York City.

The Centennial Decade Development Program was now gaining strength. Each year on Founders' Day, a program was held with a presentation of the names of alumni and friends who had placed the college in their long-range plans. October 27, 1975, was a Founders' Day that was unlike any other. This day was the kick off of Phase 2 of the Centennial Decade Development Program and on this day President Hahn announced that $1,128,000 in previously unannounced gifts, grants,

AUTHOR'S ANECDOTES

Eric, our youngest son, accompanied me to my office in Presser Hall one weekend. Next to my office was the college mailing room. Several bags of mail were in the hallway ready for the post office. Eric asked, "Daddy, are those bags full of money?" I had to tell him no there was no money in the bags, it was just mail for the post office.

and bequests had been received toward the $11,055,000 goal. The convocation was attended by students, faculty, townspeople, and other Bethany wellwishers, as well as members of the Presidents Advisory Council. The amount of $357,000 in gifts successfully completed Phase 1 of the CDDP. The remaining $771,000 dollars provided a significant thrust for Phase 2 that began that day and continued for three years.

Major gifts started to come in. The Johan E. Seleen Endowed Professorship in Religion, a $100,000 gift from Mr. and Mrs. Ernest Johnson of Marquette Kansas. Another gift was the Billue-Burnett Distinguished Professorship in Music, given in part by Syvenna Billue of McPherson, and Barbara Burnett of Lawrence, Kansas, and associated with a challenge grant of $100,000 from the Julia J. Mingenback Foundation. Both the Julia J. Mingenback Foundation of McPherson, Kansas and F.C. Thomson of Lindsborg, Kansas each contributed $100,000 toward the Thomson-Mingenback organ in Presser Auditorium. Two other smaller grants completed the fundraising for this project. One more special gift was given by Herbert Johnson, Salina, Kansas, for a much-needed maintenance facility. The Herbert Johnson Maintenance Building replaced a gym that had been moved from the Smoky Hill Air Force Base and converted into a very inefficient maintenance building.

AUTHOR'S ANECDOTES

Eugene "Gene" Mingenback was president of Farmers Alliance Insurance Company in McPherson. I heard he was very tough and people were afraid to call on him. I was young and just getting "wet behind the ears" in making development calls for Bethany, so I took a chance and made an appointment to see Mr. Mingenback. When I got to his office, I saw a businessman with long eyebrows, a loose tie, and a shirt partially unbuttoned. Gene looked at me and said "What in the hell do you want kid?" I told him I represented Bethany College and wanted to share my story. He then said, "I'll tell you what kid, I hate the Swedes." I did not give up and told my story. Then he said "God bless you—Here's a check for $200." We became close friends over time and he nicknamed me his "beggar boy." Gene and Mary Mingenback were like grandparents to me and they have been very kind to Bethany College.

Pictured Left:
Herbert Johnson Maintenance Building

Above: The day when King Carl XVI Gustaf of Sweden visited Lindsborg and Bethany College, the day before Easter, April 17, 1976. The King is in the center. To his right are Bethany College President Dr. Arvin W. Hahn, current Kansas Governor Robert F. Bennett and former Kansas Governor Robert Docking; to his left is a Kansas State Trooper.

It was in 1976 that the United States celebrated the Bicentennial anniversary of our country's founding. The city of Lindsborg thought it appropriate to invite his Majesty King Carl Gustav XVI to visit our community and college. Because of all the Swedish heritage in this valley and the college, the King accepted the invitation. Preparations for the King's visit took place months ahead of his arrival April 17, 1976. The Swedish King came to Lindsborg from Vail, Colorado where he had been skiing. It was a very quick and rushed day in Lindsborg and at Bethany College because his plane landed behind schedule in Salina. Several thousand people lined Lindsborg's Main Street as he was driven to the South Park. The town was full of security, in fact, several days earlier "manholes" in the streets were sealed and the Missouri Pacific trains were asked to go through town at a much slower speed because of the crowd of people expected for this event. The King's first stop was the Swedish Pavilion located at the historical park and near the Old Mill. This event drew a very large audience as the King rededicated the pavilion which was at the 1904 World's Fair in St. Louis, and later given to Bethany College by Sweden. It was shipped in three sections to Lindsborg and placed at its first home on the Bethany campus.

AUTHOR'S ANECDOTES

Every year I made a call on Dr. Ernest Brandsted in McPherson, Kansas for his annual gift. His office was in a home and it had a Swedish Dala Horse name sign on the front. Unknown to me, the doctor had moved his office closer to the hospital. Dr. Brandsted's son and family had moved into the old office and made it their home. The Dala Horse still hung outside the house. Thinking it was still the doctor's office, I walked right in and sat down on the sofa. Two small children were running around and it suddenly occurred to me that this was no longer the doctor's office. I left quickly and rang the doorbell. Mrs. Brandsted came to the door and I told her I had been in her house. She laughed, I apologized, and then I left for his new office.

From the Swedish Pavilion, the king was whisked to Presser Hall where the Oratorio Society chorus performed a small portion of Handel's Messiah. The King received gifts from the community, college, State of Kansas, and the Bethany students. The students presented him with a Terrible Swede sweatshirt. Security was right beside the King at all times along with the Ambassador of Sweden to the US, H. E. Count Wachtmeister. Before leaving, there was a smorgasbord in the Pihlblad Memorial Union with special guests. Seated with the King was the Kansas Governor and Mrs. Bennett. It was a short, fast, and important visit for the community and Bethany College.

In 1977 Greg Lundstrom, a new graduate of Bethany College, was added to the Public Affairs staff as Associate Director of Annual Funding. Also, Mr. Harry Ylander, 1950 Bethany College graduate, was appointed as Chief Financial Officer for the school. William Taylor, who had been Business Manager since 1952, continued with the same title, having supervision over purchasing, secretarial employment, food service, campus bookstore, building and grounds.

Founders' Day 1977 marked the completion of Phase II of the CDDP and centered around a dedication recital for the new Thomson-Mingenback Organ. It was at this time president Hahn announced an anonymous gift of $1 million for the endowment fund. Oscar D. Nelson, Kansas City, established a $100,000 professorship in business, and Elmer F. Pierson,

Top: Organ namesakes Mary Mingenback and Carl Thomson
Bottom: Thomson-Mingenback Organ in Presser Hall

Stroble-Gibson Centennial Center

Kansas City, established a $100,000 professorship in music. The number of endowed professorships now numbered five.

More building was to take place. An addition to the Ray D. Hahn Physical Education building was provided for and named after Syvenna Billue, McPherson, Kansas, who made the largest gift thus making new dressing rooms, a classroom, and weight room possible. This addition would soon have an attachment, a facility called The Stroble–Gibson Gymnasium. Also, The Miller Offices for Student Affairs, in the Pihlblad Memorial Union, were provided by Mr. and Mrs. Clair Miller, McPherson, Kansas.

On October 27, 1977, Phase III of this nine years Centennial Decade Development Plan was kicked off in Presser Hall Auditorium, with the goal of $4,015,000. Dr. Hahn announced to the convocation, including the President's Advisory Council and recent donors, that the individual goals inside this total need was $1,815,000 for the academic

AUTHOR'S ANECDOTES

It was Labor Day in the 1970s when I finally got Mrs. Olson to make a decision on the proposal I had presented to furnish the lounge in Gregory Hall for $20,000. I had the paperwork with me for the signature and was going to pick up the check. Mrs. Olson's eyesight was not good she said, "Let me fix you a cup of coffee." She had a coffee pot and only boiled water to pour onto instant coffee. I sat down at the kitchen table waiting for the coffee. Remember, Mrs. Olson's eyesight was not good. Next came in the boiling water, heading for my cup, but it missed. The boiling water went directly on my suit pants between my legs but I couldn't leave now because I had to get the pledge card signed and get the check. I jumped up slowly and went to the refrigerator for ice cubes. The ice cubes were covered on top with little fuzzies, they had been in the tray for a long time. I did get enough ice out of the trays to rub on my legs to make the burn feel better. After I got the mission accomplished, I went straight to the hospital. Since it was a holiday, no businesses were open to help me with my burns except the hospital. I had an aunt who was a nurse at the time and I told her about my problem. Aunt Mabel said " drop your drawers," and I did. I had blisters on the inside of both legs. I went back to campus and told Dr. Hahn that I needed to collect combat pay on some of our calls.

program, $200,000 for faculty development, and $2,000,000 for endowment needs. Leadership for this final phase included Jack Carlin, Lindsborg, Chairman of Area Gifts Committee; Chet Lemon, Dallas, Texas Chairman of Major Gifts Committee, and Ronald Philgreen, Shawnee Mission, Kansas, Chairman of the Deferred Gifts Committee.

Another milestone important to the college was reached at this time as well. This year, 1977, marked the fourth consecutive year that the budget for the college had been reached! Closing out 1977, Mrs. Grace Gregory, Lyons, Kansas, agreed to a major gift toward construction of a much needed new residence hall. Gregory Hall was funded with several other private gifts along with government funding. As Lane Hart Hall, the oldest residence hall on campus, built in 1883 was closed in the spring of 1978 (taken down 1983), it was with the comforting knowledge that a new hall, Gregory would be built the same year.

A good start to the 1979-1980 academic year was the announcement of a $100,000 Milfred Riddle McKeown Professorship in Science and the John Paul and Helen Louise Rohm Distinguished Professorship in Sociology and Social Service. It was at this time that the previously mentioned Stroble-Gibson Campus Center, which was attached to the side of the Syvenna Billue addition of the Ray D. Hahn Physical Education Building was completed. Funding for this addition came from two Lindsborg families, Mr. and Mrs. George Gibson and Mr. and Mrs. Jim Stroble. The Levins, another Lindsborg family, funded the Levin Dining Room in the Pihlblad Memorial Union.

AUTHOR'S ANECDOTES

Just a side note in light of the growth in men's and women's sports. Dr. Ted Kessinger said after pushing this Swede football winning streak to 29 consecutive wins,"We're thankful Swedes." Meanwhile, Jim Krob, head track coach, was assisting individual faculty and administration in the search for improved conditioning. Krob was responsible for leading the Kansas Conference in track. The Wichita Eagle wrote, "the Terrible Swedes Aren't; They're No. 1"

Above: Gregory Hall

Below: Article Clip from The Bethany Magazine, Fall 1979

LEFT:
Dr. Hahn and Mr. and Mrs. Jim Stroble study plans for the Campus Center.

ABOVE:
Mr. and Mrs. George P. Gibson.

ABOVE: Esther and Fritz Levin are greeted by President Arvin Hahn at the dedication luncheon for the new Levin Dining Room, in the Pihlblad Memorial Union.

Another highlight for Bethany College's Centennial was the live television broadcast of Handel's Messiah direct from Presser Hall Auditorium. This Easter presentation was seen by a national television audience from coast to coast. This was the first time viewers throughout the nation had a chance to tune in on the sights and sounds of the Bethany College Oratorio Society. The 3 p.m. April 19th performance was telecast live by KPTS, Channel 8-Wichita, and beamed via satellite to other PBS stations around the country. Production costs were $75,000 and underwritten by F.C. Thomson of Lindsborg, the Dane Hansen Foundation of Logan, Kansas, the Hess Foundation of McPherson, Kansas and $15,000 from alumni and friends of Bethany. The three-hour live broadcast included a brief mini-documentary about Lindsborg, Bethany College and the Messiah Festival. Several million viewers saw and heard Bethany's presentation in every state of the union

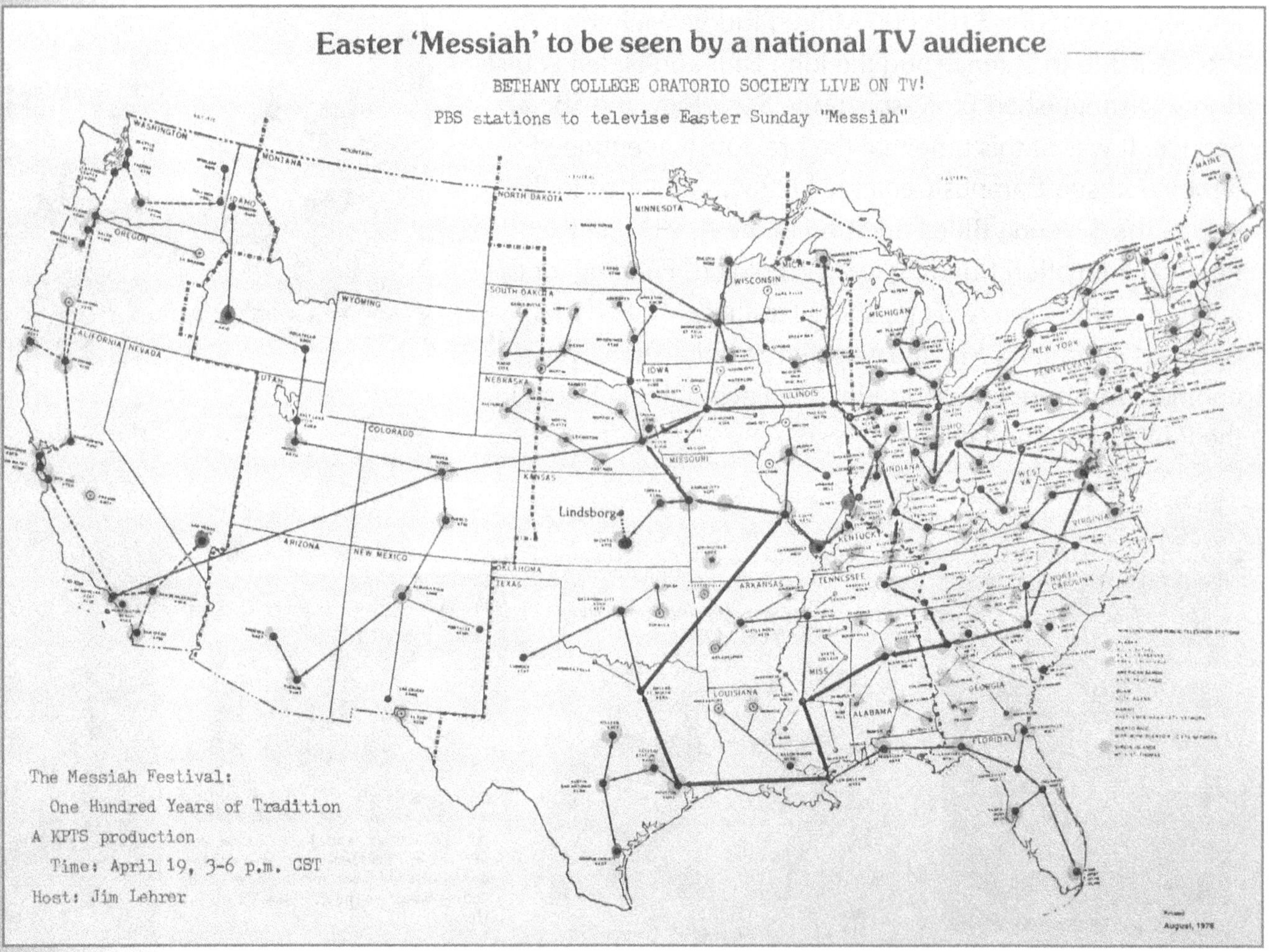

Easter 'Messiah' to be seen by a national TV audience

BETHANY COLLEGE ORATORIO SOCIETY LIVE ON TV!
PBS stations to televise Easter Sunday "Messiah"

The Messiah Festival:
   One Hundred Years of Tradition
A KPTS production
   Time: April 19, 3-6 p.m. CST
Host: Jim Lehrer

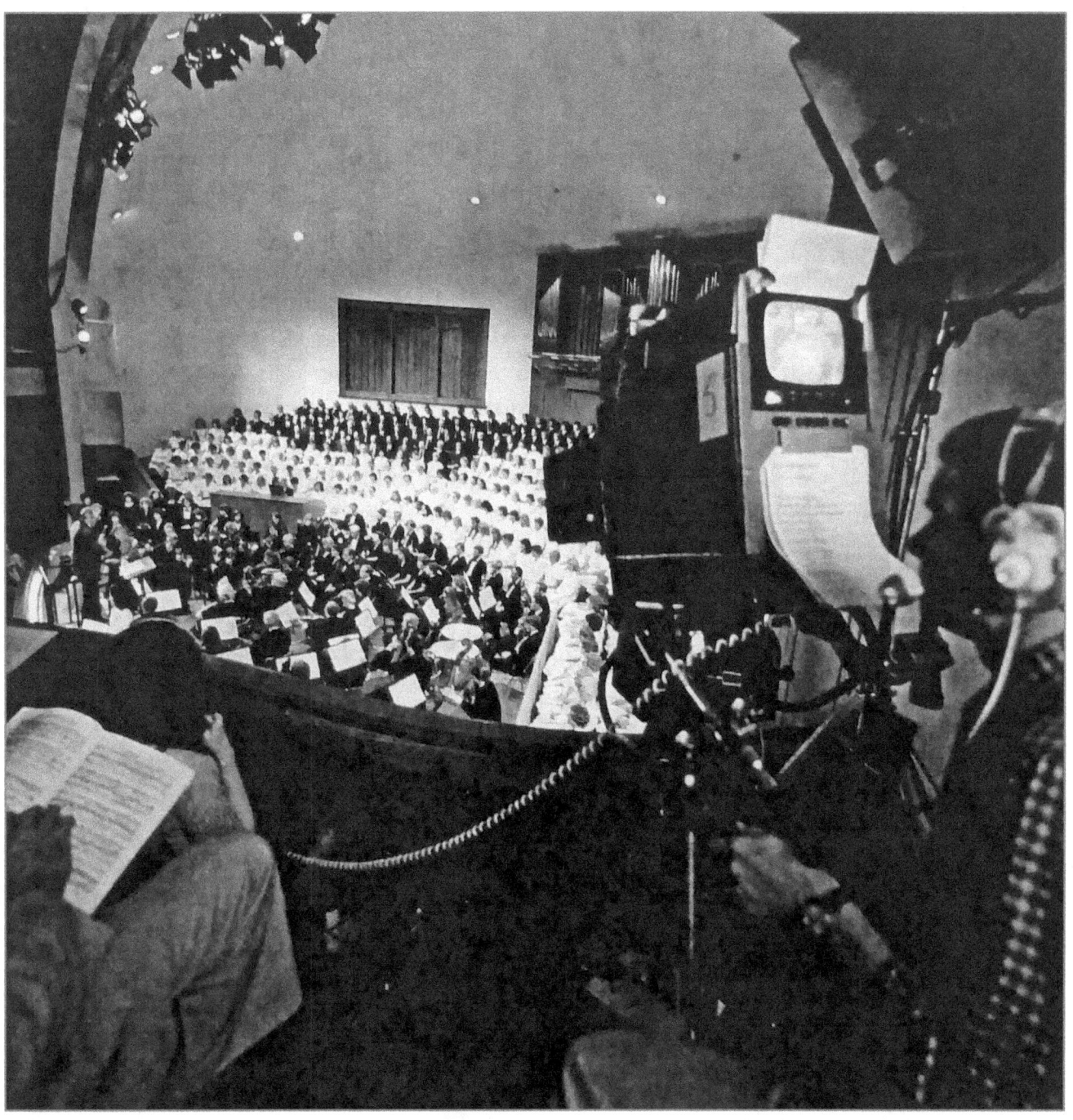

and Puerto Rico. The Iowa Public Television programmer refused this airing and received many phone calls from alumni and friends. Professor Elmer Copley, who had been at the college since 1960, directed the Messiah. The production team of Terry Lickona and Allen Muir, producer and director of the PBS series, "Austin City Limits," were in charge of the arrangements for this project. Jim Lehrer of "The MacNeil/Lehrer Report", a nightly PBS show, was the on-camera host. Lehrer, a Kansas native, attended the festival in 1943 as a member of the Wichita Boys' Choir.

The final kick off dinner of the Centennial Decade Development Program was held on April 20 and 21st to raise the final $2,500,000 and complete the nine year program. At the kickoff President Hahn announced seven gifts totaling $550,000 including $200,000 dollars from the Mabee Foundation of Tulsa, Oklahoma, $100,000 in pledges from the student body, $100,000 from the Ludvig and Selma Nelson Trust of McPherson, $25,000 from the faculty, and $25,000 from Mr. and Mrs. Carl Oakleaf of Lindsborg. The student's gift was pledged overwhelmingly for the Stroble-Gibson Center over a 10 year period from their activity funds.

This year, 1980, Bethany received a pledge of $250,000 to endow the Johnson Lectureship series. The Central States Synod of the Lutheran Church in America, and Mr. and Mrs. Charles Dean Johnson each pledged $125,000. The 124 churches in the Synod voted unanimously for the lectureship funding. Both Mr. and Mrs. Charles Dean Johnson (Lucy Peterson) attended Bethany and graduated in 1944. Following graduation from Bethany, Charles went on to earn a law degree.

AUTHOR'S ANECDOTES

Additional gifts were raised to complete the funding towards the Mr. and Mrs. Gene Burnett major gift. There was a need for a pipe organ in the Swensson Chapel. Mary Mingenback, McPherson, and Barbara Burnett were on the President's Advisory Council and they became very dear friends. Mary called and asked, "Ken, do you think Barbara would care if I purchased the pipe organ for the Burnett Center?" I assured her that Barbara would be thrilled.

Bethany Makes a Miracle

Bethany College at Lindsborg began its 101st year, earlier this month, about $15 million richer than it was a decade ago. A Centennial Decade Development Program launched in 1972 brought in not just the $11,800,000 in new funds campaign planners originally sought, but a total — as of Oct. 15 — of $15,026,000. What a way to start a new century!

Because inflation has a way of reducing the buying power even of contributed funds, Bethany's leaders wisely chose to put the funds to work as soon as they came in. So now the college's new wealth is reflected not so much in terms of an impressive bank balance as in new and improved campus facilities, a larger faculty — including the occupants of several recently endowed professorships — and a strong endowment fund.

The same day successful completion of the development program was announced, a new Stroble-Gibson Centennial Center was dedicated. This contains facilities for large gatherings, social and recreational activities personal physical fitness development. There are, for instance, two new racquetball co for which there was no room in the cam gym. The campaign made possible installa of a new pipe organ in Presser Hall, f which last Easter's performance of " Messiah" was telecast nationally. All told least 10 major new buildings have been ad to the campus in the past 14 years — mos them since the centennial fund drive star

When the campaign was initiated near decade ago, the college was in financial stra and Bethany's new president, Dr. Arvin Hahn, said it was time to try to "make a m cle." The miracle has been made.

Bethany and its 900 students and thousa of alumni and supporters who made the m cle possible deserve Kansans' congratulati

Bethany Centennial Celebration

The CDDP had now come to a close with $15,026,000 raised bypassing the original goal of $11,055,000 over a nine year period. Bethany College was 100 years old (1881-1981) and it was time to celebrate! A Birthday Party for the college took place in the Stroble-Gibson Centennial Center with 500 alumni, friends, educators, government officials, the college faculty and the CDDP leadership team all together thankful for the job well done. Four of the five living Bethany presidents were special guests at our celebration. In attendance was Dr. Emory Lindquist, Dr. Robert Mortvedt, Dr. L.Dale Lund, and Dr. Arvin Hahn. Regrets were received from Dr. G. Kenneth Andeen. The Birthday Party lasted for 12 months with featured speakers.

Four of the five living presidents of Bethany College were special guests at the Centennial Celebration. Pictured above left to right are Dr. Arvin Hahn, Dr. L. Dale Lund, Dr. Robert Mortvedt, and Dr. Emory Lindquist. Regrets were received from Dr. G. Kenneth Andeen. The 100th Bethany birthday took place over 12 months with featured speakers.

AUTHOR'S ANECDOTES

I happened to have the gift for the king of Sweden in my car and I was to get it to Dr. Hahn at the Pihlblad Memorial Union during the smorgasbord. Remember, the trains were too slow down during the king's visit, and I happened to be on the wrong side of the tracks. It took forever for the train to pass through town. Finally, my wife and I arrived at the student union where the college president was a nervous wreck. I told Arvin I could not get there any faster.

On September 15, 1982, Dr. Arvin Hahn submitted his resignation as President of Bethany College, to be effective August 1, 1983. Dr. Cloy Miene, Chairman of the Bethany Board of Directors, stated, "Dr. Hahn has served this college with unusual ability for the past 16 years." Dr. Hahn felt his resignation was at a natural breaking point following the completion of the college centennial.

AUTHOR'S ANECDOTES

Of all the different personal experiences working with the college presidents, Arvin Hahn beats them all. Arvin was a "car buff." When we were together on a trip, after completing a day of making calls, we headed for car dealerships! I sat in the backseat of new cars and used cars while the sales people went over all the details and gave him a brochure and their calling card. Can you guess how many dealerships I was in during my 16 years of working with the Dr. Hahn? Just one car was ever purchased on our trips.

Dr. Peter Ristuben 1983-1990

Dr. Peter Ristuben became the ninth president of Bethany in the summer of 1983, and assumed his duties on August 1st. He came to the college from Empire State College in Buffalo, New York, where he served as Academic Dean. He and his wife Nina had three grown children.

As the director of public affairs, I had made my decision that the 1983 – 84 academic year would be my last year of employment at my alma mater. In August 1983, I submitted my resignation to be effective in June 1984. After completing a major nine year campaign entitled the Centennial Decade Development Program, I felt it was time to step down as Director of Public Affairs and turn the reins over to new blood. Over the years I had a dream to open a business on Lindsborg's Main Street. I wanted to open a Scandinavian workshop and gift store to be called "The Hemslojd". My wife Marilyn went along with this move in our lives. Together with our partners, Kenneth and Virginia Swisher, we opened the doors for our business in August 1984.

I had a very interesting year with Dr. Ristuben. I immediately discovered he loved art, and was a very particular person. His plans for Bethany were also quite pricey. Bethany was not ready for his spending habits. During Ristuben's administration, Bethany added Lindquist Hall to the Wallerstedt Library. This addition had many features including study areas, offices, and a large conference room for college meetings and banquets. Bethany's food service provided many large banquets in this very nice setting.

In my position, it was important for me to take the president around to meet our alumni and friends. We went on an extended trip to Arizona and California where we had several appointments. Our first call on this trip was with a 1914 alumnus, Mrs. Hedvig Beckstrom in Tempe, Arizona. Mrs. Beckstrom was 80 years old and had fixed a special lunch for the three of us. For some reason Dr. Ristuben rented his own car so I wasn't with him on this particular day. Lunch was ready and Mrs. Beckstrom and I were visiting about her future major gift to her alma mater. Lunch was to be served at noon, but there was no president. It was difficult for me to make an excuse for him; he forgot to show up for lunch and our first appointment in his honor.

We went to Sun City, Arizona, to meet with Dr. Bernard Malm, who retired as president of DeSoto Coating Corporation near Chicago. Dr. Malm was an alumnus of Bethany and I had known him for several years so we reminisced about many of his friends back in Lindsborg. After the meeting, Dr. Ristuben shared with me he felt Dr. Malm shared more time with me than him and he felt slighted as president. We traveled on to Los Angeles for more alumni meetings and the president was very well received at these visits.

A gift in excess of $3 million, the largest single trust gift ever donated to Bethany College, was announced on March 2, 1984 in a town hall meeting in Presser Hall Auditorium. The gift, a donation made by the Ludvig and Selma Nelson Religion, Educational and Charitable Trust, was announced by Robert Wise, McPherson, Kansas, Attorney and President of the Trust on behalf of the trustees.

In his announcement, Wise stated Bethany College and its relationship with the Trust over the past 35 years already has resulted in over $650,000 being received by the College. In response to this announcement, President Peter Ristuben said, "this is another historical milestone in the history of Bethany College."

The donation at this time was the result of the termination of the trust agreement set forth by the Nelsons in 1948, and Bethany College was the only chairtable institution mentioned in the trust agreement by the Nelsons.

Time was marching on and I would soon be leaving a place that had been very important to my entire family. I was concerned because I believed Dr. Ristuben's taste for the very best placed Bethany in a precarious financial position. Unfortunately, Dr. Peter Ristuben died of a heart attack on January 17, 1990.

Dr. Richard Torgerson (Acting President) 1990-1991

Dr. Joel McKean 1991-1996

Dr. Joel M. McKean became the 10th president of Bethany in the summer of 1991. McKean graduated from Gettysburg College and earned his PhD in mathematics from the University of Pittsburg. He served 30 years in the United States Air Force, retiring as a Brigadier General. He and his wife Carol had four children.

As Bethany's tenth president, Dr. McKean took the ambitious step of having his development staff and community leaders work on funding for the current operating budget. He was very appreciative for all of the help he received because several thousand dollars were raised during this special effort. Dr. McKean's leadership skills from his years of service in the Air Force were reflected in his leadership at Bethany College. In 1996, however, he retired and left Bethany to focus on many areas of volunteer work.

Rev. Christopher Thomforde 1996-2000

Rev. Christopher M. Thomforde became the eleventh president of Bethany College in the summer of 1996. He came to Bethany from Susquehanna University in Pennsylvania. He received his BA degree from Princeton University, and a Masters of Divinity Degree from Yale University. Thomforde was an honorable mention All-American in basketball while at Princeton. Christopher and Christine had four children.

Rev. Thomforde, as the 11th president of Bethany, was also the tallest president to ever lead the college standing 6'9" tall. He was an outstanding speaker and preacher and his delivery always seemed to be "off the cuff." Senator Bill Bradley spoke at Thomforde's Inauguration while he was a Democratic contender for the United States Presidency. Both men were All- American basketball players while at Princeton. I was asked to pick up the senator at the Wichita Air Terminal. I wore a Bethany sweatshirt so the senator could easily identify me. Once off the plane, Senator Bradley remarked that he was hungry so we went directly to Wendy's but they had just closed and would not let us inside. Next, we tried McDonald's and we were able to get his hamburger and Coke. It was an hour drive back to town and the Thomforde's home where these two giants sat, with their shoes off, drinking chocolate milk and talking over their basketball days.

We made several calls together on friends and alumni throughout Central Kansas and on one occasion we went to Minneapolis, Minnesota for prospect calls. Although Thomforde liked to have fun, he was known to have a bit of a temper. I always told him if someone upsets you when we are making call, start to count to 10. If you are still upset go for 100!

Dr. Paul Formo 2001-2006

Dr. Paul K. Formo became the twelfth president of Bethany College coming from Dana College where he served as Vice President and Dean of Academic Affairs. He earned his master degree and doctorate from the University of Iowa. Dr. Formo and his wife Pat had two children.

Dr. Formo came to Bethany College with a music background in higher education. He was a gentle, quiet and very personal man. I felt Dr. Formo was more comfortable and preferred a one-to-one situation rather than being in a larger group. During his presidency, the campus started to take on a new look. We did make some calls together so I could introduce him to many of our friends and alumni and some new doors were opened because of our past friends. While at Bethany, he worked very hard and did a great job of keeping the operating budget in-line.

On one occasion, we met with one of our former board members, and he suggested we visit with a friend of his who might have an interest in making a gift to Bethany College. The appointment was made and we arrived at his office on time at 1:00 p.m. This was a first-time visit with this individual. He was very busy and after 20 minutes, we left with a major pledge to $250,000 to be made over a five-year period. Needless to say we were both ecstatic over this gift.

Dr. Formo and his wife retired in Iowa.

Dr. Robert Vogel 2006 (6 months)

Dr. Robert Vogel served as interim president on two occasions at Bethany College. He graduated from Wartburg College and Wartburg Theological Seminary in Waverly, Iowa. He became the Wartburg College President and served in that position for eighteen years. Dr. Vogel and his wife Sally had two children.

Dr. Robert Vogel served as interim president for the first time for 6 months. In his short time we became friends; we were the same age. Dr. Vogel brought a certain upbeat feeling to the students as the search committee looked for the next president.

Dr. Vogel did ask for assistance on several occasions and I had the opportunity to help in the Advancement Office. The campus took on a nicer look during Vogel's short time of service and anyone who had not been here for several years would have noticed the changes.

Dr. Edward Leonard III 2007-2015

Dr. Edward Leonard III became the 13th president of Bethany, coming from Wilmington College in Ohio, where he served as Vice President for Advancement. Leonard graduated from William Jewell in Kansas City, received his MBA from Saint Louis University, and his Doctorate from the University of Missouri in Kansas City. He and his wife Sheila had two sons.

Once again I did make a few calls with Dr. Leonard to make introductions. Dr. Leonard, along with the staff and Board of Directors, placed in motion a long range program for the 130th anniversary of the college in 2030. Enrollment did increase along with contributions. The sale of $6 million in bonds financed through the Kansas Independent College Financing Authority, and other gifts, funded three major building projects and provided funds necessary to complete the Campus Green Project. These funds were used to complete a large laboratory addition and renovate the front entrance to Nelson Science Hall, add a weight room and additional space for coaches' offices, and build "Swede Suites," a three story apartment style student housing addition for 67 students. The Campus Green Project completed new walkways, resurfaced parking lots, added a promenade of flags, Stolz Circle, a limestone amphitheater and

Nelson Science Center

Stolz Circle

remodeled east entrance to the campus which included a Welcome Pavilion. In 2014 Bud Pearson, Storm Lake, Iowa made a $1,000,000 matching challenge gift to the school to build a chapel designed similarly to those in Sweden. Another major gift, naming the interior of the chapel, was $250,000 from Lucy, the wife of Charles Dean Johnson, McPherson, Kansas. This area was named after Rev. Johan Seleen, a grandfather of Lucy's husband Charles. Attached to the chapel was the Mabee Welcome Center. The Mabee Foundation of Tulsa, Oklahoma, made a gift of $500,000 to also be matched by the college. Several alumni and friends made this facility possible. The Mabee Welcome Center would house

"Swede Suites" student housing

New Hall

offices, meeting rooms and the Office of Student Admissions. Bethany also benefited from the charitable estate of Clyde and Glenn Lindstrom from Falun, Kansas. The College and Smoky Valley USD 400 received $700,000 which replaced the sod on the shared football field with artificial turf. One additional facility was constructed during the Leonard presidency, a new dormitory, that would be situated on the campus where the former Deere Hall stood. Things were happening, but Bethany was not financially healthy.

Leonard resigned on June 5 to accept the presidency of Birmingham University, in Alabama. Provost Macur had already resigned his position May 29 and accepted the presidency at Medaille University in Buffalo, New York. News came out soon after our leaders had resigned that the National Higher Learning Commission had placed Bethany on probation giving the college until the 2017 fiscal year end to get it's house in order!

Pearson Chapel & Mabee Welcome Center featuring the "Delphi" sculpture donated by Sid Stolz in 1983 and housing the Spirit Bell and Admissions Office

Dr. Robert Vogel 2015-2016

Bethany College was very fortunate to have Dr. Robert Vogel return with his expertise for the second time as interim president. Vogel and his wife Sally left Denver to make their home in Lindsborg for one year.

Vogel appointed Dr. Robert Carlson, business professor, to be interim provost. Galen Bunning, Vice president for Advancement soon left to accept a position with Kansas State University. Now there was a need for an interim Director of Advancement as well. Dr. Vogel approached me to see if I would consider a position as supervisor of the Advancement Office. After some thought and visiting with my wife Marilyn, we made a decision. I accepted the challenge to take on this position for a 10 month period. It really was not an ask, but calling. When I was director of development in the 1960s, we went through a similar problem. The 60s challenge was met and the college turned around to a positive position. I wanted this to happen again and discovered raising funds for Bethany had not changed much over the past six decades!

Our advancement team was very lean to begin plans to raise $4 million over a two-year period. During this special effort we needed a representative that knew and loved their alma mater living on the West Coast. Bethany was fortunate to have Leon Burch, 1964 graduate, living in Vancouver, Washington. He gladly became this important addition to the advancement office and made calls on west coast alumni. Burch was a former director of admissions and colleague of mine during the Arvin Hahn Administration.

Under Vogel's leadership, a two year campaign entitled "Investing in Student Success" was quickly put into action for gifts and pledges directed toward balancing the annual operating fund. The advancement staff included Warren Olson, Associate Vice President of Advancement, 1972 graduate, Molly Johnson, 2006 graduate, Director of Alumni and Annual Funding, Alisa Jones and Jane Asche.

First on the agenda was to set up the Lindsborg Community Leadership consisting of 12 leaders who would help by making calls on the first tier of our community campaign. While this group was completing their calls, approximately 100 other workers had their calls to make. Dr. Vogel, Leon Burch, and the advancement staff made hundreds of calls–many personal; some by letter, during the 2015 – 2016 fiscal year. The College was very fortunate to receive several major gifts for this effort.

Will Jones
14th President of Bethany College

The City of Lindsborg, Lindsborg Community Hospital, Lindsborg Community, alumni and friends from all over the United States, invested in this very important campaign. At the end of the 2015 – 2016 fiscal year, June 30, our first year goal was met with over $2,000,000 in gifts and pledges. Other gifts were on their way to help reach the final goal by June 30, 2017.

While the campaign was in progress, another important committee was in motion. In October 2015 a presidential search committee began meeting with the intention of having a new president by July 1, 2016. In the spring of 2016, the three chosen presidential candidates were interviewed by representatives of the College and community. The position of the 14th Bethany College president was offered to Will Jones, LaGrange, Georgia. My last month of full time work in the Advancement Office was spent with Will Jones during his first month as president in July of 2016. Bethany College is very fortunate to have Will, Amy and the Jones family in the Lindsborg community. Dr. Vogel's work was done, Leon Burch's work was done, and I, once again, retired from Bethany.

During the year that Dr. Vogel worked to stabilize Bethany, before the new president arrived, the Campus Ministry Team composed a prayer that resonated throughout the community and was used often. I thought it appropriate to include this prayer.

Prayer of Bethany College 2015-2016

Spirit of the Living God,
    gather us from near and far,
    generation upon generation,
    campus and community,
    into one common purpose.

Call us to courage:
    meeting difficult truths with innovation,
    and matching faith in your guiding wisdom
    with diligent labor of mind and body.

Call us to reverence:
    increasing our trust in one another,
    and tempering our determination
    with gentleness of heart and tongue.

Call us to excellence:
    rising beyond our self-imposed limitations
    to the impossible abundance that you have always promised,
    and to the privilege of stewardship for all who enter our halls.

In Jesus the Christ,
    who calls ordinary people to extraordinary service
    especially when we least expect it:
    may it be so, now and always.

Amen.

Photo & Scrapbook Extras

Rev. Dr. Carl Aaron Swensson
Bethany Founder & 2nd President
1889-1904

Edward Nelander
1st Bethany President 1882-1889

Rev. Dr. Ernst Frederick Wilhelm Pihlblad
3rd Bethany President 1904-1941

Carnegie Library
Built 1908
Burned down December 1981

Lane Hart Hall
Built 1883
Demolished 1983

Mr. & Mrs. Mark Schupbach
Mark 1971 graduate,
Marty 1969 graduate
with Mr. & Mrs. Wallerstedt

Mary Mingenback, Arvin Hahn, and Kenneth Sjogren

Accepted March 1967

March 1967 - Back to Bethany to work

SOUTHERN ILLINOIS UNIVERSITY
CARBONDALE, ILLINOIS
CERTIFICATE OF ADMISSION

GRADUATE SCHOOL __x__ YEAR __1967__ QUARTER __Fall__ RECORD NO. __513286655__
DEGREE __MA__
MAJOR FIELD __Higher Education__

ENTRY STATUS:
☐ Illinois Resident   ☐ Re-entry
☐ Continuing   ☒ Graduate
                      ☒ New Graduate
Comment __1__

NAME __Mr. Kenneth E. Sjogren__
STREET __747 North Second__
CITY & STATE __Lindsborg, Kansas 67456__

This form shows that you have fulfilled the entrance requirements to Southern Illinois University. Please present this card at the Graduate School when you register.

Mrs. Sharon Bruckerpt   3/22/67
DIRECTOR OF ADMISSIONS   DATE

FORM 2-40636-7

Press Conference with Advisory Council

Swensson Statue
Founder of Bethany College

"The Terrible Swede" Statue 2014
by Dick Bergen, 1953 Graduate

THE Bethany College MAGAZINE

SUMMER 1980

THE Bethany College MAGAZINE

VOLUME 75, NO. 3 / Lindsborg, Kansas / SUMMER ISSUE 1980

EDITORIAL

Our Bethany Centennial — A Time For Reflection and Regeneration

Two activities need to take place if Bethany's Centennial is to be a success. These intellectual undertakings may be referred to under the general themes of reflection and regeneration.

On the matter of reflection, there will be many happenings during which the past ought to and will be revisited.

Among the most significant times for such occasions will be the Homecomings of 1980 and 1981 and the Messiah Festival in the spring of 1981. In addition there will be the several alumni meetings at Easter and at the end of the academic year in 1981, as well as the group get-togethers which are now being planned for various locations throughout the country during the next fourteen months. All of these ought well be times for amusing and valued reflection. There'll be replay of stories about yesterday's scholarly notables, and these will be cast in the best of prose.

However, with only reflection the Centennial would not be complete! Stated another way, should we tend to ride into the future on the catapult of yesterday alone, our ride will be less than fulfilling.

We must while reflecting also borrow from the futurists. We must add our interest and concern about energy, about our understanding of the role of the new computer languages, about our involvement in Third World Issues — as well as our constant search for improved conditions among all of humanity. Such a cast into the depths of our second century's opportunities, while not divesting ourselves of yesterday, will indeed aid in the preparation for an improved future.

My hope and prayer are that we will be good distillers of the very valuable things which should never be lost from yesterday, while on the other hand my expectation is that we will be intelligent refiners of the ideas and experiments of those who are looking at tomorrow. This, I hope, will ultimately bring a broad array of ideas both past and future onto the campus and into the programs of Bethany, to be used as valued resources by our faculty and students.

Without question the Centennial year ought indeed to be exceptional. Do help make it exceptional by joining us in the many significant Centennial occasions during 1980 and 1981.

Together with this message please also accept my most sincere gratitude for your interest and support in the past and my hopes for our continued merit of that support in the future.

—ARVIN HAHN, President

THE BETHANY MAGAZINE/Summer 1980 Page 2

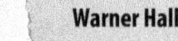
Warner Hall

Hahn Physical Education Building
Newly Built

Architect Concept Art of Pihlblad Student Union

E.T. Anderson Memorial Courts demolished in 2018 to make room for 6 new courts in memory of Emory Lindquist.

Sjogren Center Alumni Office 1986 - 2016

May- 27. 77

Sirs:—

I will have ninety thousand dollars available after Dec. 20-77. Would contribute it toward a scholarship fund if it would be taken off Income Tax. Please let me know so as to make arrangements for investment if this isn't possible.

Respect,

Mrs. Grace Gregory
114 E. Truesdell
Lyons, KS 67554

Lindquist Hall

Bethany College 1886

www.ingramcontent.com/pod-product-compliance
Lightning Source LLC
Chambersburg PA
CBHW081349040426
42450CB00015B/3369